Macro-economic Thinking and the Market Economy

An essay on the neglect of the micro-foundations and its consequences

L. M. LACHMANN
Professor of Economics and Economic History,
University of the Witwatersrand, Johannesburg,

1949–1972

Published by
THE INSTITUTE OF ECONOMIC AFFAIRS
1973

Printed in Great Britain by
TONBRIDGE PRINTERS LTD,
Peach Hall Works, Tonbridge, Kent
Set in Monotype Baskerville

PREFACE

The *Hobart Papers* are intended to contribute a stream of authoritative, independent and lucid commentary to the understanding and application of economics. Their characteristic concern is the optimum use of scarce resources and the extent to which it can be achieved by markets within an appropriate legal and institutional framework. The first 50 were published from 1960 to 1970. The second 50 in the 1970s will continue the central study of markets and of the environment created by government.

The interest in the working of markets explains the essentially micro-economic approach, i.e., the study of individuals, families, firms or other small homogeneous groups as buyers and sellers.[1] Several *Hobart Papers* have been the work of distinguished economists who have used the technique of macro-economics, i.e., the study of the behaviour of aggregates such as national income, expenditure and production. Economics comprises micro and macro elements but their relationship is rarely clarified. Since the 1930s economists who have followed the some 40-year-old approach of J. M. Keynes have often appeared to say, or to think, that macro- has replaced, or is superior to, or is distinct from, micro-economics. And this confusion has for many years been translated into some text books and into 'popular' writing for laymen. Professors Armen A. Alchian and William R. Allen's *University Economics*,[2] which should be better known in Britain, puts macro-economic analysis of fluctuations in employment, national income and output in its place as 'relying on the basic theorems of micro theory'.

In *Hobart Paper No. 55*[3] Mr Douglas Rimmer illustrated the misleading results of the unthinking application of macro-economic concepts to the developing countries. In this *Hobart Paper* the methods of thought and analysis of macro-economics and leading macro-economists are further examined by Professor L. M. Lachmann to see how far they yield valid hypotheses about human activity and prescriptions for

---

[1] Economic analysis can also be applied to giving and receiving: *The Economics of Charity*, IEA Readings No. 12, 1974.
[2] Wadsworth Publishing, Belmont, California, 3rd edn., 1972; in the UK, Prentice-Hall International, Hemel Hempstead, Herts.
[3] *Macromancy: The ideology of 'development economics'*, IEA, April 1973.

policy. He divides macro-economics into two main schools: the first, the neo-Ricardians, led in Cambridge (England) by Professors Joan Robinson, Piero Sraffa, and Nicholas Kaldor, and the second, the neo-classical school, represented mainly by Professors Paul Samuelson, Robert Solow and Sir John Hicks. In a recent article[1] Professor James Tobin is highly critical of the Cambridge School in England and defensive of Cambridge in the USA; in this *Paper* Professor Lachmann is severely critical of both. He finds the analyses of both schools defective on the ground that they have lost sight of the micro-economic foundations of economic behaviour. Although those economists who seem to be critics of the Cambridge School claim to have inherited the micro-economic approach of the neo-classical economists such as Leon Walras and Vilfredo Pareto, Professor Lachmann argues that they have not fully incorporated the essentials of neo-classical economics and that their thinking is no less defective than that of the Cambridge School.

To go to the roots of these fundamental differences in the thinking of economists, Professor Lachmann has had to conduct a highly theoretical discussion that will be easier for economists than for beginners or for non-economists. The more fundamental the differences, and the arguable errors, in economic thinking, the more abstract the reasoning must be. If macro-economists have been using poor reasoning and emerging with bad recommendations, it is essential to re-examine the fundamentals of their methods. There is no easy way to grasp their conclusions without an effort to understand how and why they think as they do. This *Hobart Paper* is therefore more theoretical than most have been, but newcomers to economics and laymen will find it rewarding if they persevere in their effort to understand it, perhaps in a second or third reading, because the implications for policy could be radical.

If Professor Lachmann is right, much of the thinking of economists for the last 40 years has misled a generation or two of students, teachers, popularisers of economics in the press and broadcasting, businessmen and politicians. For the inference would be that macro-economics has a useful rôle to play in economic thinking and policy only if its underlying micro-economics are understood. It is safely used by economists who are constantly aware of the substructure of individual decisions

'Cambridge (U.K.) v Cambridge (Mass.)', *The Public Interest*, Spring 1973.

in buying and selling; it is unsafe in the hands of economists who think it *replaces* the substructure, or that it is sufficient to assume that individuals, or individual entities like families and firms, will act in the way that conforms to macro-economic laws, rules, tendencies or generalisations typically made about the behaviour of large groups such as a country, an economy, or a society as a whole.

The reader who masters Professor Lachmann's analysis will find that the implications for policy are indeed far-reaching. Professor Lachmann briefly indicates the erroneous conclusions that have been drawn from macro-economics for current policies in the Western countries: the control of incomes and wages as a means of mastering inflation, the management of economic growth, ensuring technical progress, and the monetary policy required for a progressive, open society.

Professor Lachmann's analysis is scholarly but the implications of his approach are revolutionary: for the teaching of economics, for the authority with which economists offer advice, for the respect in which they are held by industry, government and society in general.

The Institute would like to thank Professor Armen A. Alchian and other economists for reading an early draft and offering comments and suggestions which the author has taken into account in his final revisions. Its constitution requires it to dissociate its Trustees, Directors, and Advisers from the analysis and conclusions of its authors; but it offers Professor Lachmann's study to economists of all schools, and to non-economists who benefit or suffer from their thinking and advice, as a reasoned re-assessment of a school of thought which has dominated economics for decades.

June 1973   EDITOR

THE AUTHOR

L. M. LACHMANN was born in Berlin in 1906 and studied in Berlin and Zurich. In 1930 he obtained the degree of *Doctor rerum politicarum* from the University of Berlin. In 1933 he came to England where he did research work in economic theory at the London School of Economics and held the Leon Research Fellowship in the University of London from 1938 to 1940. He was Acting Head of the Department of Economics of the (then) University College of Hull from 1943 to 1948. In 1949 he went to South Africa as Professor of Economics and Economic History in the University of the Witwatersrand, Johannesburg. He retired at the end of 1972. He was President of the Economic Society of South Africa from 1961 to 1963 and has been a member of its Council since 1950.

Professor Lachmann's publications include *Capital and its Structure* (Bell, 1956); *The Legacy of Max Weber* (Heinemann, 1970); articles in the learned journals, particularly 'Economics as a Social Science' (Inaugural Lecture), 1950, 'The Science of Human Action' (*Economica*, November 1951), 'Mrs Robinson on the Accumulation of Capital' (*South African Journal of Economics*, June 1958), 'Sir John Hicks on Capital and Growth' (*South African Journal of Economics*, June 1966); and contributions to *festschriften* for eminent economists, especially 'Methodological Individualism and the Market Economy' in Erich Streissler *et al.* (eds.), *Roads to Freedom: Essays in honour of Friedrich A. von Hayek* (Routledge & Kegan Paul, London, 1969), and 'Ludwig von Mises and the Market Process' in *Toward Liberty* (Institute for Humane Studies, Menlo Park, California, Vol. II, 1971). Most of these writings are concerned with the analytical foundations of the market economy and the question of how far modern economics provides an adequate picture of it.

CONTENTS

[7]

GLOSSARY

ARBITRAGE—action by which different prices for the same good in different markets are brought to uniformity, e.g. by London stockbrokers buying a share in Paris and selling it in London whenever the Paris price is lower than the London price.

EX ANTE—EX POST (before—afterwards)—economic actions look different when they have happened from what they did when planned.

EXCHANGE ECONOMY—an economy in which existing goods are exchanged but no production takes place.

FORMALISM—a style of thought according to which abstract entities are treated as though they were real. Contrast with SUBJECTIVISM (page 10).

HOMOGENEITY—HETEROGENEITY ('MALLEABILITY')—an aggregate, such as a capital stock, may consist of elements that are all alike like drops of water in a lake. If so, it is homogeneous, otherwise heterogeneous.

INVESTMENT DECISION, SPECIFYING—a decision to build a house or ship involves turning an amount of money into a concrete and *specific* object. This decision cannot be reversed.

KALEIDO-STATICS—'The economy is in the particular posture which prevails, because particular expectations, or rather, particular agreed formulas about the future, are for the moment widely accepted. These can change as swiftly, as completely, and on as slight a provocation as the loose, ephemeral mosaic of the kaleidoscope. A twist of the hand, a piece of 'news', can shatter one picture and replace it with a different one.' (G. L. S. Shackle, *A Scheme of Economic Theory*, Cambridge, 1965, p. 48.)

LEARNING BY DOING—learning from practical experience rather than from books or lectures. Technical knowledge acquired in the workshop. *It takes time.*

MALINVESTMENT—investment which turns out to be a failure, yields less profit than was expected. *See also* EX ANTE—EX POST.

MARGINAL EFFICIENCY OF CAPITAL—'The relation between the prospective yield of a capital-asset and its supply price or replacement cost, i.e., the relation between the prospective yield of one more unit of that type of capital and the cost of producing that unit, furnishes us with the marginal efficiency of capital of that type.' (J. M. Keynes, *General Theory*, p. 135.)

NEO-CLASSICAL PRODUCTION FUNCTION—a neo-classical theorem in which total output is regarded as a function of total input of capital and labour, one that yields constant returns to a proportionate increase in all the inputs.

One version is the

COBB-DOUGLAS FUNCTION—a linear homogeneous production function, in which the elasticity of substitution between capital and labour is always one.

PRODUCTION ECONOMY—an economy in which, as distinct from an exchange economy, goods have to be produced as well as exchanged.

SUBJECTIVISM—The postulate that all economic and social phenomena have to be made intelligible by explaining them in terms of human choices and decisions. Contrast to FORMALISM (above).

TECHNICAL PROGRESS—is said to be *embodied* when each new invention requires a new 'machine' to give it expression. It is *disembodied* when its results can be incorporated into all old machines so that the age of a machine has no effect on its efficiency.

TECHNICAL PROGRESS FUNCTION, KALDOR's—a macro-function that makes the *results* of technical progress dependent on the rate of gross investment (below, p. 45).

TECHNOCRATIC APPROACH TO CAPITAL THEORY, SOLOW's—'Solow classifies capital theories as either technocratic or descriptive. They are technocratic when planning and allocation questions (and so socialism) are discussed, descriptive when used in an explanation of the workings of capitalism.' (G. C. Harcourt, *Some Cambridge Controversies in the Theory of Capital*, Cambridge University Press, 1972, p. 93.)

WELFARE ECONOMICS—'Welfare economics is the study of the well-being of the members of a society as a group, in so far as it is affected by the decisions and actions of its members and agencies concerning economic variables.' (D. M. Winch, *Analytical Welfare Economics*, Penguin Modern Economic Texts, 1971, p. 13.)

I. INTRODUCTION

In our day the market economy is under relentless and heavy criticism. Some of these criticisms are due to ignorance. Some show a remarkably high degree of skill and sophistication. This *Paper* is devoted to a critical evaluation of some of the more sophisticated ideas deployed in this debate.

'A multitude of perspectives'

Nobody can claim, of course, that the market economy can be viewed only in one kind of perspective superior to all others, that it requires for its full understanding an analytical scheme of its own, or that any particular body of thought can be said to 'represent' it. In the study of the social world there is a good deal to be said for a multitude of perspectives and styles of thought, each of them illuminating one aspect of the problem under investigation. It remains true none the less that some of these perspectives are apt to blur essential features of the object of study and to distort our vision. In such cases we are entitled to state that some styles of thought are inadequate to their subject matter.

In what follows we shall endeavour to show that such inadequate styles of thought are prominent in a contemporary debate among economists in which the nature of the market economy, the way it works and the results it achieves, are at issue.

II. THE GRAND DEBATE

For almost two decades now a controversy has raged on the higher levels of economic theory, particularly in capital and growth theory, which concerns some essential features of the market economy, but in which those human actions which give rise and lend meaning to these features are ignored. From time to time the contestants will address to one another requests to 'state your assumptions clearly', but these injunctions always seem to apply to macro-economic variables, such as incomes, output or investment, used here as instruments of combat; they never extend to the types of action, the plans of millions of

[11]

consumers and producers, the mostly unintended results of which these variables are meant to symbolise.[1]

The 'Cambridge' and 'neo-classical' schools

This is by no means the only curious feature of the situation in which the controversy takes place. One of the contestants, the 'Cambridge School', as we shall call it, is strongly critical of the market economy. In their view, the mode of distribution of the national income between wages and profits is indeterminate, which means that profits are not an 'economically necessary' type of income and, in practice, might almost indefinitely be squeezed with impunity by taxation. To be sure, retained profits are necessary for economic growth, but the payment of dividends, and indeed any consumption by non-workers, are regarded as unnecessary![2] We might call this school of thought 'post-Marxist', were it not that to Marx and Engels the very idea that the mode of income distribution under capitalism is indeterminate would have been abhorrent.

Strictures on the market economy are, of course, nothing new. During the centuries of its existence they have come from many sides and been made on many occasions. But so far the market economy also has always found ready exponents on many sides and many levels, in particular among the most eminent economic thinkers of each age. When around the turn of the century what came to be known as the 'Neo-classical' school of economic thought gained prominence, two of its outstanding thinkers, Pareto and Gustav Cassel, devoted a good deal of their efforts to espousing the market economy and launched some vigorous critiques of collectivist ideas. Eugen von Böhm-Bawerk whom, as an 'Austrian', we should perhaps not include in this school, stood on the same side.

[1] A book of readings containing excerpts from most of the important contributions to the debate has recently been published in the Penguin Modern Economics Readings. It provides an excellent introduction to it: G. C. Harcourt and N. F. Laing (eds.), *Capital and Growth, Selected Readings*, Penguin Books, 1971. Joan Robinson, *Economic Heresies. Some old-fashioned questions in Economic Theory*, Macmillan, 1971, is virtually in its entirety a contribution to the debate; also J. A. Kregel, *Rate of Profit, Distribution and Growth: Two Views*, Macmillan, 1971.

An almost point-by-point commentary on the various issues at stake in the debate is in G. C. Harcourt, *Some Cambridge controversies in the theory of capital*, Cambridge, 1972. To the serious student it is indispensable. The author hides neither his sympathy for the Cambridge side nor his lack of sympathy for the market economy.

[2] Cf. the note on David Ricardo, below, p. 17, footnote 4.

What is odd about the present situation is that while the Cambridge School assails essential features of the market economy, their opponents, who have borrowed the name 'neo-classical', have shown no strong desire to accept this part of their inheritance, viz. to espouse the market economy. To be sure, their claim to the neo-classical inheritance is not uncontested. Professor Joan Robinson always refers to them as the 'neo-neo-classical' school. But it is clear that such eminent contemporaries as Professors Paul Samuelson and Robert Solow, while certainly regarding themselves as the heirs of Leon Walras and Vilfredo Pareto, do not wish to incur these liabilities of their inheritance. Perhaps to their way of thinking such liabilities do not exist.

The reasons for this attitude are not to be found in scholarly reticence towards the affairs of one's own day and age. Professor Solow felt no compunction recently in denouncing the pretensions of a good deal of what goes by the name of 'radical economics'.[1] Professor Samuelson has never been known for undue reticence when it comes to letting the world know his views about this or that topical question. In successive editions of his famous textbook he has, indeed, given such matters increasing space and attention.

The reasons are partly to be found in the degree of remoteness of the 'model' which forms the shell of their thought from the everyday processes of the market, a remoteness of which they cannot but be well aware, but partly in a strange weakness, an unwillingness to challenge the basis of their opponents' thought.[2]

In the first place, the neo-classical model assumes perfect competition, which in our world hardly exists, though in the industrial economy of the 19th century the predominance of the wholesale merchant in most markets produced results not altogether dissimilar from it. Furthermore, within the body of thought that came to be known as welfare economics[3] and in which some members of the neo-classical school have come to take an interest, a prominent place is occupied by the notion of a 'Pareto Optimum', an 'ideal' general equilibrium position based on perfect competition, free access to all markets and equal knowledge shared by all participants. Anybody feeling committed to this 'ideal' would naturally compare the

---

[1] *American Economic Review, Papers and Proceedings*, May 1971, pp. 63–65.
[2] C. E. Ferguson gives a concise and polished statement of neo-classical views in *The Neo-classical Theory of Production and Distribution*, Cambridge, 1969.
[3] 'Glossary', p. 10.

market situations of the real world with it and find them wanting. In this way our judgement on the world as it is comes to depend not merely on the world as we would wish it to be, which is quite proper and, in a sense, inevitable. It comes to depend on a comparison with a fictitious state of equilibrium of which nobody has as yet explained how it could come about in reality. After a few strenuous exercises in the manipulation of the macro-variables of our model, such as incomes, output or investment, the question of which *human* actions keep them in being vanishes from sight, and we may permit ourselves to establish the fictitious world of our model as a criterion by which to judge the world as it really is. Clearly, however, this enchantment with welfare economics cannot be regarded as a complete explanation of the attitude of the neo-classical school to the market economy.

The controversy takes place in a strange mental atmosphere. The strangeness is not entirely due to the level of abstraction, high as it is, on which the two rival schools move. It is often said that what is a permissible level of abstraction depends on the problem at hand, and that every thinker must be allowed to exercise his discretion in such matters. This may be so, but until recently two rules have generally been observed in this context. The first, which Cassel in particular used to emphasise, is that from the initial level of abstraction, however high, it must be possible gradually to approach reality by a sequence of approximations involving the modification of the initial assumptions. At the very start of an argument it has to be decided which assumptions will be modified later on and which will not. The second rule concerns what may be abstracted from and what not. Essentials fall into the latter category. In discussing a system of action, for example, we are not entitled to abstract from the springs of human action, the purposes sought by individuals and the plans in which they find their expression, by assuming their *modus operandi* to be known and therefore predictable. The strange character of the atmosphere in which our controversy takes place owes not a little to the fact that these two rules are more often honoured in the breach than in the observance.

Assumption of macro-equilibrium
The two rival schools of thought conduct their argument within the context of *macro*-economic equilibrium. This

means that the economic forces the mode of interaction of which is at issue are long-term economic forces reflecting the movement of certain economic *aggregates*, like investment or exports, of *apparently* unchanging composition. The field of motion of these forces is the 'economic system' as a whole. The *micro*-economic origins of these forces are not under discussion by our two rival schools. The relevance of these assumptions to the working of the market economy whose operations they are, after all, supposed to reflect calls for some immediate comment.

In the real world there is no equilibrium, although there certainly are equilibrating forces of various degrees of strength and speed of operation. They operate with varying degrees of ease in different spheres. They encounter obstacles of various kinds. In general we may say that the more swiftly the co-ordinating forces can do their work the stronger the chance that a state of equilibrium will be reached. Thus, in the large international financial markets in which *arbitrage*[1] is worth while, and as long as capital movements are unhampered, equilibrium may be established within a matter of hours. On the other hand, where durable and specific capital goods play a prominent part in markets, the attainment of equilibrium becomes precarious because it may take a long time before they fall due for replacement, and meanwhile new changes will probably affect other elements of the situation.

Needless to say, but as we shall have to emphasise repeatedly, macro-economic equilibrium, i.e., equilibrium of the economic system as a whole, is a more problematical concept than market equilibrium. Equilibrium of the individual, household or firm, is a much simpler notion than either and is virtually synonymous with rational action. Everybody knows from experience that he cannot hope to succeed in a course of action unless he is able to co-ordinate the various acts of which it consists. Consistency of plan is always a necessary condition of success. The smaller the micro-unit the more firmly based is the concept of equilibrium. We must not forget that whenever we pass from the sphere of action controlled by one mind, in household or firm, to the sphere of action in which diverse minds have to take their orientation from one another while each is pursuing its own interests, as in a market, we face a formidable array of problems of the existence of which all too many economists

[1] 'Glossary', p. 9.

[15]

seem blissfully unaware. To discuss a problem within a general equilibrium context must mean to pin one's faith on the over-riding strength of the equilibrating forces operating in the situation under discussion. By the same token, one must regard what obstacles there may be in the path to equilibrium as surmountable, and disequilibrating forces as too weak to disrupt the result. But how do we know that in every such encounter the equilibrating forces will, in the end at least, always gain the upper hand?

The neglect of the micro-economic foundations of aggregate magnitudes, on the other hand, means that the game is being played with a set of macro-variables as chips into whose origins, i.e., individual actions, we must not inquire. What is more important, we have to take the constant molecular composition of the chips, the unvarying numerical magnitude of the aggregates, for granted. The macro-variables, to be sure, will be affected by the operation of one upon another, within the field of equilibrium forces, but never, it seems, by forces operating within each one of them. It is easy to imagine what will happen if theories based on such assumptions are applied in circumstances of rapid unexpected change, in which the continuous constant composition of the aggregates, e.g., outputs produced by various industries, can by no means be taken for granted.

We shall call the style of thought which finds its expression in assumptions such as these and which is common to both our contending factions *macro-economic formalism*.[1] We may speak of formalism whenever a form of thought devised in a certain context, in order to deal with a problem existing there and then, is later used in other contexts without due regard for its natural limitations. We shall try to show that this is precisely what has happened to the concept of equilibrium in the economic thought of our age.

III. MACRO-ECONOMIC FORMALISM AS A STYLE OF THOUGHT

Though the style of macro-economic formalism finds its expression in the writings of both our rival schools, they have come to acquire it in different ways and evidently do not

---

[1] 'Glossary', p. 9.

equally feel at home in it. We cannot fail to notice that members of the Cambridge School wield these weapons not only with much more confidence but also with more competence and verve. We may suspect that one reason at least for the dexterity with which we see them handle the instruments of macro-economic formalism has to be sought in the circumstance that these enable them to dispense with individuals, the differences between their minds, and the inequality of men in general. Their opponents, the neo-classical Samuelson-Solow school, prompted by no such desire, may have embraced this style of thought for other reasons and probably in a mood of innocence, but cannot escape the consequences of their choice. Having embarked upon it they helplessly drift further and further away from the micro-economic shore.

The Cambridge School has repudiated the marginal revolution of the 1870s and regards *subjectivism*,[1] the style of thought to which we owe marginal utility and expectations, as at best an aberration. Professor Joan Robinson on the first page of the Preface to *The Accumulation of Capital* says that

'Economic Analysis, serving for two centuries to win an understanding of the Nature and Causes of the Wealth of Nations, has been fobbed off with another bride—a Theory of Value'.[2]

Mr Piero Sraffa, the Cambridge School's most original thinker, who has provided the inspiration for the work of most of the others, gave his book the characteristic sub-title *Prelude to a Critique of Economic Theory*.[3]

A. THE 'NEO-RICARDIAN' COUNTER-REVOLUTION

The members of the Cambridge School are best described as latter-day Ricardians.[4] For the reason given above we cannot call them post-Marxists. They prefer the label of neo-Keyne-

[1] 'Glossary', p. 10.
[2] *The Accumulation of Capital*, Macmillian, 1956, p.v.
[3] Piero Sraffa, *Production of Commodities by Means of Commodities. Prelude to a Critique of Economic Theory*, Cambridge University Press, 1960.
[4] David Ricardo (1772–1823) endeavoured to find an invariable measure of value, i.e. a common denominator to which all economic phenomena could be reduced, in the same way as in daily life we use pounds and pence, but that would not be distorted by inflation and deflation. He thought it could be found in labour, because all goods and services require hours of work to come into existence. This labour theory of value was never quite satisfactory, even

Continued on page 18

sians, but we may have misgivings about that. Keynes, for all his interest in macro-economics, owed little to Ricardo and all his life remained a subjectivist[1] who refused to cast the inducement to invest in the mould of a macro-variable such as the acceleration principle. He disclaimed any interest in long-run equilibrium and substantiated this disclaimer by pointing out that in the long run we are all dead.

The main aim of the present-day Cambridge School appears to be an attempt to undo the results of the marginal revolution and to bring about a Ricardian counter-revolution. For a hundred years economists have taken it for granted that what happens in a market economy ultimately depends on the subjective preferences and expectations of millions of individuals finding expression in the supply and demand for goods, services and financial assets. If we accept this approach we are compelled to pay close attention to the differences between human preferences and the divergence of expectations. If not, we are presumably free to turn our attention to facts supposedly 'socially objective'. In a world in which differences of preferences and divergence of expectations do not matter there is, of course, no room for entrepreneurs.

To neo-Ricardians the distribution of incomes, admittedly a Ricardian term, appears to have no meaning except within the narrow terms of 'classes of the community'. How incomes are, for example, distributed among capital owners does not seem to interest them. That people belonging to the same 'class' may act in many different ways in the same 'objective situation', that there can be no competition without some competitors being unsuccessful while others are successful—all these are facts not congenial to neo-Ricardian thinking. For them econ-

[1] 'Surmise and assumption about what is happening or about to happen are themselves the *source* of these happenings, men make history in seeking to apprehend it. This is the message of the *General Theory*.' (G. L. S. Shackle, *The Years of High Theory*, Cambridge, 1967, p. 130.)

Continued from page 17

to Ricardo himself, but Karl Marx took it up with some ardour. He asked how, if labour is the only source of value, there can be profits, i.e. an income going to non-workers.

In the 1870s economists came to see that not labour but utility is the source of value, that how many hours of work a good required has little to do with its value, and that value is not an objective quality inherent in goods and services but a subjective quality bestowed upon them by the appraising mind of the buyer.

omic action always means the response of a 'typical agent' to a 'given' situation. Men act exclusively in their capacity as 'workers', 'capitalists', or 'landlords'. Spontaneous action does not exist. Men do not really *act* in the Ricardian world, they merely *re-act* to the circumstances in which they happen to find themselves. It is thus hardly surprising that the neo-Ricardian understanding of the ways in which a market economy functions is somewhat limited, and subjectivism is seen as nothing but an aberration from the true path of economic thought. Ricardo can be said to have thought essentially in long-run equilibrium terms. So it is not surprising to find that macro-economic formalism is a style of thought congenial to his latter-day disciples.

Lip-service to micro-foundations

From time to time, though, we find that lip-service is paid to the micro-foundations of economic phenomena. The return to the classical style of thought requires a strenuous effort, and a century of subjectivism has understandably left deep traces in the minds of our would-be Ricardians which they appear unable to erase completely. We even find the truth occasionally acknowledged that macro-equilibria require causal explanation in terms of human choice and decision.[1]

But these admissions are never permitted to affect their analytical practice. When it comes to explaining economic processes we are usually told, for example, that 'entrepreneurs' make investment decisions, 'rentiers' place their wealth in one form or another, while consumers consume what is left of the GNP. Stereotypes play the part of economic agents. Economic events are the result of some kind of collective process of decision-making the *modus operandi* of which is never explained. Imaginary beings take the place of real people.

---

[1] 'To build up a causal model, we must start not from equilibrium relations but from the rules and motives governing human behaviour. We therefore have to specify to what kind of economy the model applies, for various kinds of economies have different sets of rules. (The *General Theory* was rooted in the situation of Great Britain in the 1930s; Keynes was rash in applying its conclusions equally to medieval England and ancient Egypt.) Our present purpose is to find the simplest kind of model that will reflect conditions in the modern capitalist world.' (Joan Robinson, *Essays in the Theory of Economic Growth*, Macmillan, 1962, p. 34.) The reader will not fail to notice, even here, the somewhat ambiguous characterisation of the springs of action as 'rules and motives'. Which are the more important?

Salvation by econometrics?

The attitude of their neo-classical opponents to macro-economic formalism is much more difficult to describe. As Walrasians they can hardly be oblivious of the micro-foundations of macro-theory. Was not one of Walras's achievements precisely this, namely, to have fused economic events on the level of individual, market, and system within one body of thought, and to have found in the notion of equilibrium the unifying concept, the instrument which permits us to view micro- as well as macro-economic phenomena as elements of an organic whole? But the strength of prevalent intellectual fashions is not easily resisted, their admiration for Keynes and his work is strong (most of them like to think of themselves as Keynesians), and the ease with which Keynesian macro-variables, such as employment or investment, appear to lend themselves to statistical measurement have induced them to look to econometric investigations as a means of verifying their theories. Indeed, the more hard pressed by their opponents, the more they have become inclined to look to the econo-metricians for their ultimate vindication. The attempt, on the one hand to cling firmly to acts of choice and decision as the foundation of economic phenomena, while at the same time presenting one's theories in an 'operationally meaningful', i.e., statistically measurable, form has naturally turned out to be a source of weakness which their opponent neo-Ricardians have not failed to exploit.

Macro-formalism adopted by both schools

Hence the two rival schools have come to embrace macro-economic formalism as their common style of thought for different reasons, the Cambridge School from inner conviction, the neo-classicals dazzled by the brightness of Keynesian success. From this difference there has followed a difference in attitude towards mode of verification and realism of assumptions. The neo-classical formalists are inclined to regard realism of assumptions as less important so long as they permit us to make 'testable predictions'. For a long time they evidently regarded the conformity of statistical series in the USA and elsewhere to the *Cobb-Douglas function*[1] as empirical evidence for

[1] 'Glossary', p. 10.

the neo-classical theory of distribution.[1] Professor Solow in his De Vries Lectures[2] of 1963 drew on statistical series for such corroboration, and in his *Growth Theory*[3] (1970) does the same to support the notion of 'steady growth'.

Naturally their opponents have of late turned their fire on these weak positions. Thus Professor Joan Robinson has shown that, precisely in so far as neo-classical theory is firmly based on micro-foundations, is grounded in, and meant to lend expression to, individual acts of choice and decision, it defies statistical verification.

'Statisticians can find out in a rough general way, for a particular situation, the capital-output ratio in dollar values and the share of profit in the dollar value of net output, so that they can estimate the overall *ex post* rate of profit on capital. They cannot describe what was in the minds of directors of firms or on the drawing boards of engineers when the choices were made which led to the creation of the existing stock of capital equipment. Still less can they say what choices *would*[4] have been made if the rate of profit had been different from what it is.'[5]

Her criticism here is directed, it is true, against only one of the neo-classical positions, namely, the so-called 'neo-classical production function'.[6] But it clearly must extend to any theory based on individual choice between alternatives. The more firmly a macro-economic argument is linked to its micro-foundation in choice and decision, the less it lends itself to statistical verification. Since the range of choice present to the minds of decision-makers defies statistical measurement, no theory linking observable events, like output quantities or

---

[1] A rather precarious position to take. 'The conclusion must be that the fitting of the Cobb-Douglas function to time series has not yielded, and cannot yield, the statistical realisation of the production function. It can describe the relations between the historical rates of growth of labour, capital, and the product, but the coefficients that do this do not measure marginal productivity.' (E. H. Phelps-Brown, 'The Meaning of the Fitted Cobb-Douglas Function', *Quarterly Journal of Economics*, November 1957, p. 551.)

[2] Robert M. Solow, *Capital Theory and the Rate of Return*, North Holland Publishing, Amsterdam, 1963, especially pp. 72–93.

[3] R. M. Solow, *Growth Theory. An Exposition*, Clarendon Press, Oxford, 1970.

[4] Italics in original.

[5] *Economic Journal*, June 1970, p. 336. The reader will not fail to notice, we trust, what an effective use, in the heat of combat, our eminent neo-Ricardian is making of an argument which spells pure subjectivism! A century of it has left its mark even in the minds of our Ricardian counter-revolutionaries.

[6] 'Glossary', p. 10.

prices, to choice and decision is, in this sense, 'testable'. The circumstances influencing decisions find their mental reflection in plans. All economic action is, in the first place, the making and carrying out of economic plans. So long as there are no statistics of plans there is nothing to which the econometricians can correlate their measurements.

A theory couched in *equilibrium* terms cannot be tested by measurements taken in a world of continuous *disequilibrium*. Any hope that the disequilibrating forces, from which in our theory we have abstracted, would in the real world operate in such a fashion as to offset one another and produce a net result of zero and so yield equilibrium, is evidently quite unfounded in reason or experience. In the real world in which statisticians have to work, some markets will be in equilibrium at any moment, others in disequilibrium. Thus *the 'economic system as a whole' is never in equilibrium*. How can statistical measurements taken in such circumstances either verify or falsify equilibrium theories of the neo-classical type?

The Ricardian shadow

The Cambridge School, in pointing out the weaknesses of the methodological position of their neo-classical opponents, have done nothing to strengthen the foundations of their own. Of course they are unable to jump over their Ricardian shadow. Expectations do not fit into their analytical scheme and have to be kept at arm's length. The variability of human preferences, shaped by experience and guided by the diffusion of knowledge from one individual to another, from market to market, from country to country, is best ignored, though, to be sure, its consequences cannot always be. For Ricardians the consumer does not exist at all. Theirs is a world of production and distribution. Consumption is not an economic activity. Consumers' demand has no effect on prices. For the neo-classical formalists he does exist, but his is a rather shadowy existence. Only his preferences, permanent by assumption, not the course of his actions, are considered to be of any interest to economists. Once his preference scales have been fully recorded he is dismissed into the realm of shadows and told never to come back. It is characteristic of the formalistic style of thought that those who have imbibed it become incapable of conceiving of spontaneous human action, as distinct from reaction to outside events.

[22]

We shall attempt to show that in this controversy both the Cambridge and the neo-classical schools are prevented by their equilibrium preconceptions from understanding the nature of the market processes of reality. They are tempted to regard as 'macro-variables' what are in reality the cumulative results of millions of individual actions. Since these micro-economic actions are not necessarily repeated from day to day, even less from year to year, we have no reason at all to believe in the aggregative constancy of the macro-variables over time.

B. A BRIEF HISTORY OF THE CONTROVERSY

Stage 1

The controversy began in 1953 with a frontal attack by Mrs Robinson on the 'neo-classical production function' as a macro-variable designed to show output as a function of labour and capital input.[1] She showed that there is no such thing as a quantity of capital, hence no measurable input of it. In 1956, she presented a model of a theory of growth (with and without technical progress) without measurable capital.[2] Some awkward corners were encountered there which the eminent author managed to turn with elegance and ease. Expectations were effectively disposed of by assuming that everybody always expected the future to be like the past. The effects of changes in consumers' demand were obviated by the assumption that the stock of capital always had (but how?) exactly that composition required by the composition of the 'bundle' of consumption goods consumers demanded. Though the possibility of malinvestment, thus considerably restricted in any case, was candidly admitted to exist all the same, we were given to understand that, by and large, the current capital stock represented the cumulative result of all the investment decisions taken down the centuries. Capital was heterogeneous, and thus not measurable, but this heterogeneity had no effect on the process of accumulation.

Stage 2

The next stage was reached in 1960 with the publication of Mr Sraffa's book.[3] The atmosphere of Ricardian long-run equilibrium is here all-pervasive. From the first page to the

[1] Joan Robinson, *Collected Economic Papers*, Blackwell, 1960, Vol. II, pp. 114–131.
[2] *The Accumulation of Capital, op. cit.*
[3] *Production of Commodities by Means of Commodities, op. cit.*

last we find ourselves in a world in which every market is always in equilibrium. No word is wasted on telling us how such equilibria might in reality be attained or what would happen if they were disturbed. His most important conclusion is the indeterminate character of the distribution of incomes between wages and profits in such a model. The instruments of marginal analysis were blunted. From this conclusion it further followed 'that there is no such thing as a "quantity of capital" which exists independently of the rate of profit'.[1]

In Chapter XII of his book, 'Switch in Methods of Production', Mr Sraffa discussed the possibility of using the same method of production at more than one rate of profit. This gave rise to what came to be known as the 'Reswitching Controversy', which the neo-classical side for a time regarded as the heart of the matter but which we can now see to have been a mere episode. We shall therefore deal with it very briefly. Here the Cambridge School won a clear victory. They were able to establish that, as Mr Sraffa had said, techniques of production are not uniquely related to 'relative factor prices'. The same technique of production may be the most profitable to use at a lower as well as a higher rate of profit, while others may be more profitable at an intermediate range. We are therefore not entitled to assume a continuous variation in techniques of production consequent upon changes in the rate of profit, e.g., in such a way that as the rate of profit falls more and more 'capital intensive' techniques will be chosen. In principle a return to a technique formerly used at a higher rate of profit is always possible. Whether it will really occur depends on the technology available. Thus the same water pump which was the most profitable to use when the rate of interest was 9 per cent may again be the most profitable at 5 per cent while others are more eligible between $5\frac{1}{2}$ and $8\frac{1}{2}$ per cent. The neo-classical side had originally denied this possibility.

Stage 3

Of late the controversy has taken a new turn. The turning point is clearly visible in Dr Luigi Pasinetti's famous article of 1969.[2] The opening passage unambiguously indicates the real aim of his attack.

---

[1] Joan Robinson, *Collected Economic Papers*, Blackwell, 1965, Vol. III, p. 13.
[2] L. L. Pasinetti, 'Switches of Technique and the "Rate of Return" in Capital Theory', *Economic Journal*, September 1969. The opening passage is on p. 508.

'Whenever a new result emerges, in any theoretical field, it is natural to look back on traditional theory to verify whether, or to what extent, received notions may still be used or have to be abandoned. The outcome of the recent discussion on the problem of switches of technique seems to have started a process of this kind for the analytical tools used in the theory of capital.'

The Cambridge School, throughout the period on the offensive, now attempts to show that the rate of interest (or profit) is as indeterminate within the neo-classical system as it is within Sraffa's neo-Ricardian model. They assert that, contrary to Professor Solow's view, no such rate can be found as a dependent variable within a system of equilibrium prices; that, if to be used in such a system, it has to be determined *from outside it*. For the market economy of reality it means that, since there is no marginal productivity of capital to govern the rate of profit, the distribution of incomes between profits and wages is economically indeterminate. Profits may be squeezed by trade union or government action with no untoward result, except possibly on the growth rate.

It is at this point that we must enter the fray. Profits are an essential feature of the market economy. Does the controversy cast any light on the necessity of profit? Perhaps we shall be able to illuminate some very odd aspects of the position shared by both contending schools if we attempt to elucidate the nature of profits, their function in the market economy, the circumstances which give rise to them and those which modify their magnitude.

IV. THE NATURE OF PROFITS AND 'THE' RATE OF PROFIT

There must be more than a few economists who, when reading the works of Ricardo or Marx or their latter-day disciples, have found themselves wondering where exactly we are to look, in real life, for a counterpart of the rate of profit. Workers earn wages, we are told, and capital owners receive profits. We all know where to look for the real counterpart of wages. Though wage earners earn wage-rates which may differ very much, in ordinary circumstances a wage earner of a given category may expect to earn a wage-rate of more or less given magnitude which may vary between certain, but finite, limits. With profits we have no such indication of its future magnitude at all.

Profit is the difference between the price at which a commodity is sold and its cost to the seller. Such differences may assume any magnitude, including a negative one. Losses are by no means uncommon in business, though no firm could sustain them in the long run.

Competition implies varying rates of profit

Profits are an essential feature of the market economy. Each firm attempts to maximise its profits over some period of action which may be short or long. This period may vary as circumstances change. But however the target is defined, each action must contribute towards its attainment. The firm must strive to make a profit on each transaction it enters upon. A capital owner invests his capital where he hopes to obtain the highest rate of net return. But *motivation* of action and *success* of the action thus motivated are by no means the same thing. It is possible to describe the working of a market economy in terms of the universal orientation of its active entrepreneurial minds to maximum profits; it is absurd to do so in terms of universal success. The very nature of competition, another essential feature of the market economy, renders the success of all plans impossible. Hence we find unsuccessful firms side by side with the successful, even within the same industry or region. We find malinvestment side by side with capital investments that have succeeded beyond the boldest expectations of those who made them. There is no such thing therefore as *a rate* of profit, there are only *rates* of profit which may differ widely.

This situation has, of course, something to do with the heterogeneity of capital, a property of the capital stock that plays a part in the controversy with which we are concerned, but its true significance lies beyond that of mere physical heterogeneity. If we assume all capital to be homogeneous (an assumption Keynes shared with Ricardo and Böhm-Bawerk as well as most of the older neo-classical economists) there can be only one rate of profit. But while physical heterogeneity of capital is a cause of the variety of profits we find in reality, it is not the only cause. Two completely identical machines, used in two different factories, may not be at all equally profitable to their owners. Thus even physical homogeneity does not entail a uniform rate of profit. For profit accrues in the first instance to a capital *combination*, the stock of variable composition held by a firm, and its imputation to each single component of it is often a matter of some intricacy.[1] This fact nevertheless serves further to impair the notion of a uniform rate of profit.

Long-run equilibrium is unattainable

For Ricardo, of course, the originator of the idea, the uniform rate of profit was simply a corollary of free access to all markets. If rates were different all capital would flow out of the least profitable branches of industry and accumulate in those most profitable, thus bringing about a uniform level of profitability. This is a property of long-run equilibrium. But in our world in which so much capital is durable and specific, these equilibrating forces, on the final triumph of which Ricardo relied, can operate only slowly, though of course at varying rates in different sectors of the system. When they can only operate slowly, however, it is very likely that they will be overtaken by the disequilibrating forces of unexpected change, and the long-run equilibrium position will never be reached. The faster the equilibrating forces can do their work, the more we can rely on them and *vice versa*. All this goes to show, first, how fraught with danger are all equilibrium theories when applied to a world in which the triumph of our equilibrating forces, even their final triumph, may by no means be taken for granted. Secondly, our argument shows that the structure of the capital stock in terms of durability and specificity cannot, any more than its composition in terms of the combinations mentioned above (a *micro-economic* category by any description!), be ignored with impunity, even in a macro-economic argument like that concerned with the tendency to uniformity of all rates of profit.

There are of course markets in which the Ricardian mechanism operates with great speed and success, and in which equilibrium is as a rule established swiftly and efficiently. This is naturally possible only within the general framework of the market economy. We may mention here the whole gamut of

---

[1] Discussed in some detail in L. M. Lachmann, *Capital and its Structure*, Bell, 1956, pp. 3–12.

financial markets. In the loan markets arbitrage will swiftly bring about a structure of interest rates. There is the Stock Exchange, a market for securities embodying titles to shares in capital combinations, and thus for expected future income streams, in which an equilibrium of asset prices entailing a yield equilibrium for classes of assets of the same degree of riskiness is established every day. Such yield equilibrium, however, has nothing whatever to do with what Ricardians, young and old, mean by the rate of profit. It is not identical either with Fisher's rate of return over costs,[1] the neo-classical version of the Ricardian concept. On the contrary, what happens in a market economy is that the market brings about a state of affairs in which differences in the rates of return to different types of capital (buildings, machines, stocks of goods) invested in different enterprises are offset by capital gains and losses, in such a way as to make these assets of different profitability on capital originally invested in them equally attractive to present wealth holders. The market is thus an ingenious device for letting bygones be bygones and compelling us to direct all our mental strength towards unravelling the secrets of the future. The rate of (dividend and earnings) yield on all shares to which the market ascribes an equal degree of risk has, of course, to be equal, but this says nothing about the rate of return on capital *originally* invested in them.

Inter-temporal exchange rate

We may also imagine a system of inter-temporal markets such as Keynes envisaged,[2] in which present goods can be exchanged for future goods as well as against one another. An 'own rate of interest' would come to exist in each market, but a general rate would prevail in the end in such a way that it is no more profitable to carry a stock of timber than one of coal. This general rate of interest would of course reflect the 'time preference' of the market as a whole in the same way as Stock Exchange prices reflect the degree of risk aversion or preference of the market as a whole. Again, however, this equilibrium rate of inter-temporal exchange has nothing to do with the Ricardian rate of profit. Contemporary Ricardians will hardly find

---

[1] Irving Fisher, *The Theory of Interest*, The Macmillan Co., New York, 1930.
[2] J. M. Keynes, *General Theory of Employment, Interest and Money*, Macmillan, 1936, Ch. 17.

it to their taste. Considering their hostile attitude towards subjectivism (they loathe utility and neglect expectations whenever possible), they are unlikely to grant high status to an economic magnitude reflecting time preference, another subjective attitude. The concept must be suspect to them precisely because it rests on a firm micro-economic foundation.

We may surmise, on the other hand, that this equilibrium rate of inter-temporal exchange is more or less what the neo-classical school of Samuelson, Solow, and others mean by the rate of interest. If so, two points have to be raised. First, this concept has a clear and unambiguous meaning only within the context of an inter-temporal exchange economy, but not necessarily in an economy in which time-consuming processes of production take place and durable equipment is used. In the former we may, indeed we have to, assume that stocks carried of each of our commodities are of equilibrium size. Without equilibrium stocks there can be no equilibrium price. But in an economy with durable and specific capital equipment this is hardly feasible. There must be in the stock some 'fossils'— capital goods produced long ago, in a situation quite different from today's, which would not be replaced in their present form were they to be destroyed by accident. In other words, in a production economy such as we know it the stock of capital never has its equilibrium composition. In a pure exchange economy there is no reason why it should not have it.

Solow's 'social rate of return'

Secondly, if this is what the neo-classical school mean by the rate of interest, they have not as yet said so. Professor Solow's 'social rate of return', to be sure, is an inter-temporal rate, but in a one-commodity world. Our equilibrium rate requires inter-temporal price adjustments in order to be established. In the Solovian model there are no prices that could change. Also, his rate of return appears to apply to a production, not an exchange, economy without fossils. But in a production econ-omy in which stocks are not of equilibrium size there is no place for an equilibrium rate of inter-temporal exchange.

In short, Professor Solow's model is irrelevant to the market economy. He is not unaware of it:

'It may be claimed that a capital theory erected on planning grounds has no relevance to the actual behaviour of any real capitalist economy. That argument has often been made, with considerable success, against static competitive price theory. Capital theory is unlikely to be immune to the same complaint.'[1]

It is hard to see how, then, he can on the very next page 'suppose that my point of view could be described as a modern amalgamation of Wicksell and Irving Fisher'.[2] These two thinkers were concerned with the market economy and tried to elucidate problems of investment arising within it. They never, to our knowledge, looked at them from 'the planning point of view'. They knew that in a market economy all economic changes, hence investment, in the first place find their expression in relative price-level changes. The one-commodity world as an auxiliary device, to be sure, was not unknown to them. But they knew better than to leave things there.

But this is not all. In Fisher's system the rate of return over costs is closely linked to the rate of interest which in its turn reflects time preference. It is by comparing the two that the investor decides which projects to pursue.

'Planner's approach' to investment

In Fisher's theory of interest subjective and objective elements, time preference and investment opportunities, are thus evenly matched. (Of course, even such opportunities, existing as expectations in the minds of investors, are strictly speaking subjective elements, but Fisher wrote before expectations entered modern economics in the 1930s.) Professor Solow deliberately ignores the subjective element of time preference and, choosing the 'planner's approach', concentrates on the supposedly objective investment opportunities to calculate his rate of return on investment.

The case is instructive because it highlights some characteristics of the style of thought of neo-classical formalism.

First, it bears out our contention that only lip-service is paid to the micro-economic foundations. These economists may well acknowledge, in a general way, the significance of human preferences and expectations in economic life. However, when serious problems are encountered (and for Professor Solow the

[1] *Capital Theory and the Rate of Return*, op. cit., p. 16.
[2] *Ibid.*, p. 17.

'rate of return' is the central problem of capital theory), time preference is ignored and a 'technocratic' view taken.[1]

Secondly, when confronting a serious problem in a market economy, the neo-classical mind seems unable to view it in the perspective of savers and investors, those who in reality have to solve it. It must be viewed instead in the perspective of a hypothetical planner. We conclude that economists who propound such recipes are not really interested in how the market economy functions, and that those who are have little to learn from them.

In any case, the overall inter-temporal rate of exchange provides only a floor level. Evidently no lower rate of profit is possible. To this we may add that in a loan market in which financial institutions, fairly expensive to run, are important lenders, interest rates must be high enough to enable them to cover their costs. So much, following Sir John Hicks, an eminent neo-classical economist, we may take over from Keynes's liquidity preference.[2] This provides us with another, and probably higher, floor level.

But in any normal situation in a market economy profits are, of course, considerably in excess of this level, and capital lenders will adjust their demands to what they feel borrowers are able to pay. There must, of course, be equilibrium in the loan market. The demand is governed by profits expected to be earned on capital at present completely mobile ('free capital', Cassel's 'capital disposal') when it is invested, and this in its turn depends on the constellation of price-cost differences, present and expected.

Profits are a phenomenon of disequilibrium

Profits are earned wherever there are price-cost differences. They are thus a typical disequilibrium phenomenon, impermanent, continuously shifting as regards origin and magnitude, affected by contrived change (innovation) as well as by undesigned change emanating from population movements, shifts in demand and so on. Profits are a permanent income flowing from ever-changing sources, like the profits of a restaurant in which a different set of customers chooses a different set of dishes from the menu card every day. The existence of monopoly power, however important as a source of profits, makes no

[1] 'Glossary', p. 10.
[2] John Hicks, *Capital and Growth*, Oxford University Press, 1965, pp. 286–90.

difference to our description because in the long run, with which we are here concerned, monopoly power is no more permanent than any other sources of profit.

The erosion of price-cost differences is prompted by many forces and may take numerous forms. Pressure of competition by rival sellers is by no means the only such force. Trade unions and producers of component parts and other inputs may exert pressure on profits. Consumers, swayed by the force of fashion, or for reasons of their own (e.g., boredom), may turn away from what used to be a successful product.

All this means that the magnitude of profits, in each period, is shaped mainly by short-period forces. All the time a long-run force tending to eliminate these price-cost differences is at work. In long-run equilibrium, in which by definition the equilibrating forces have finally prevailed over all the forces of disruption, there are no profits. The persistence of profits in a market economy is due to the persistence of disequilibrium in some sector of the economic system. As in a kaleidoscope, the constellation of forces operating in the system as a whole is ever changing. Like in Professor Shackle's interpretation of Keynes, *kaleido-statics*[1] rather than static equilibrium is therefore rightly regarded as the method of analysis appropriate to the reality of the market economy.[2]

Micro-foundation of profits

Two conclusions relevant to our theme follow from what has been said. First, the ever-elusive and fugitive price-cost differences which are the source of all profits can have no place in the long-term equilibrium world to which the two rival schools are both committed. *An equilibrium rate of profit is thus a contradiction in terms.*

Secondly, profits are pre-eminently a micro-economic phenomenon. Their basis is to be found primarily in the ever-changing pattern of price-cost differences in a thousand different markets. Without understanding this micro-foundation of the phenomenon we cannot understand its essence. We certainly should not be able to formulate a general theory of profits without it. A macro-economic theory of profit can therefore make little sense.

[1] 'Glossary', p. 9.
[2] G. L. S. Shackle, *A Scheme of Economic Theory*, Cambridge University Press, 1965, Ch. IV.

After these elucidations let us return to our controversy. In it two questions are at issue between the contestants. Is there a rate of profit and a rate of interest, or do the two in equilibrium coincide? And are these two rates, or is this rate, determinate?

(a) One equilibrium rate (neo-classical school)

On the first question, the neo-classicists hold that in equilibrium there can be only one such rate of return, Professor Solow's 'social rate of return', an inter-temporal equilibrium rate of exchange.[1] As we saw, such a rate, if at all meaningful in a production economy, must be based on time preference and would constitute in reality a minimum of all possible rates. The neo-classical view must therefore mean that in the long run, when all productive possibilities have been exhausted, the rate of interest is entirely determined by time preference. Such a position evidently requires a stationary economy and is incompatible with growth.

(b) Distinction between the two rates (Cambridge School)

The Cambridge School insists on a clear distinction between rate of profit and rate of interest. 'The normal rate of profit must be sharply distinguished from the rate of interest', Professor Joan Robinson tells us.

> 'The reward of waiting—the rate of return on rentier wealth—is determined in the money market. With the facilities that modern institutions provide, marketable placements are much less risky than productive assets; the level of their yields is normally much below the prospective rate of profit that attracts real investment.'[2]

She admits that

> 'The rate of profit on capital is neither uniform throughout an economy nor steady through time. Nevertheless, the concept of the normal rate of profit determined by investment and the propensities to save provides the framework of a general theory within which detailed analysis can be built up',

[1] As Professor Solow put it, 'I have some good news and some bad news for Professor Pasinetti. The bad news is that he will have to reconcile himself to the equality of the interest rate and the rate of return, because it is so'. (*Economic Journal*, June 1970, p. 427.)

[2] Joan Robinson, *Economic Heresies*, Macmillan, 1971, p. 48.

as delightful an example of macro-economic *non sequitur* as we might have wished.

The continuing separate existence of the two rates is here apparently due to the inability or unwillingness of the 'rentiers' to turn their wealth into forms which would permit them to share in the higher profits to be derived from real or 'productive' assets. It is not clear why those able to manipulate *financial* assets should, as a 'class of the community', be unable to manipulate *real* assets. If risk aversion is the answer, it has to be pointed out that this, of course, is a property of individual minds and hardly a characteristic of a social class. Can it be that another temporary lapse into subjectivism, a sin against the Ricardian spirit, has here misled our author into reaching a most un-Ricardian conclusion, namely, the continuing existence of two rates of return on capital?

Evidently the difference between the two schools on this point merely reflects a difference in the level of abstraction on which the argument is conducted. The neo-classical rate of return applies strictly only to a one-commodity world with inter-temporal exchange but no growth. As soon as we try to apply it to a production economy with change in a multi-commodity world, the unity of the rate of return vanishes. Where there are many investment opportunities appearing in succession over time there is more than one rate of return. It is true, of course, that at each moment the most profitable of them will attract all the new investment and constitute Keynes's 'marginal efficiency of capital'.[1] But even apart from this being a matter of divergent expectations, with an ever-shifting pattern of profits this magnitude, a creature of the Keynesian short run, is liable to continuous change, and the equilibrating forces tending towards a uniform rate are thus continuously overtaken by the forces of change. It is only by adhering to a level of abstraction which permits us to ignore these forces of change that we can rest confident of the final triumph of the equilibrating forces. Neo-classical formalism, for all its ostensible reliance on micro-economic foundations, is apt to find the forces emanating from them in reality frequently rather disturbing and inconvenient. The neo-classical edifice of thought is not well integrated.

The Cambridge School, on the other hand, conducts the

[1] J. M. Keynes, *op. cit.*, Ch. 11.

argument here on a slightly lower level of abstraction. The two rates are now prevented from being fused into one by what we found is a rather peculiar device: one of the equilibrium forces, that tending to bring about equality of the rate of return to real assets with the 'rate of return to rentiers' wealth', is permanently arrested. We may admire the resourcefulness of the neo-Ricardian mind in this effort at lowering the levels of abstraction, but it is clear that this phenomenon, as well as a host of similar phenomena, can be more simply and fully explained by going back to the micro-economic sources of macro-economic forces. In the real world of the market economy there is such a multitude of rates of profit and rates of interest that the possibility that they will all one day fuse into a single entity seems remote. Neither, however, is it likely that they will fuse into two such entities.

Absurdity of the 'normal rate of profit' concept

On the second question, of the determinate character of the rate or rates concerned, the opposite conclusions of the two schools really follow from the arguments set forth above. The neo-classical formalists, as the heirs of Walras and Wicksell, have little choice but to regard their uniform rate of interest as a dependent variable of their general equilibrium system. If it is not determinate, *neither is any price.*

The Cambridge School is equally committed to Mr Sraffa's demonstration that in the Ricardian system, once wages are allowed to rise above subsistence level, the mode of distribution between wages and profits, and hence the rate of profit, are indeterminate. In a growing economy, to be sure, in Mrs Robinson's words quoted above, we find 'the concept of the normal rate of profit determined by investment and the propensities to save', which presumably gives it the desired determinate character as a result of purely macro-economic forces. The implication evidently is that for the rate of profit to become determinate we require a peculiar economy, one in a state of equilibrium growth.

The notion of a 'normal rate of profit' in a growing economy is a notion even more absurd than in one without growth. Profits are a concomitant of change in a market economy. It is hard to see why growth as a type of change should be capable of engendering regular incomes of a kind which in other cases of change would be wholly absent. Devotees of

[35]

macro-economic formalism, of whatever intellectual origin, are compelled to seek reasons where there are none in order to be able to dwell on a level of abstraction where the real reasons vanish from sight.

The suggestion may be made that we interpret 'the normal rate of profit' not as a unique value, but as the 'equivalent' of a whole range of values, of all the different rates of profit earned in reality by different firms. It would 'stand for' a whole 'structure of profit rates' in the same way as for Keynes 'the' rate of interest 'stands for' the whole structure of interest rates. But this suggestion in no way serves to resolve our dilemma.

First, the Ricardian argument requires a unique value of the rate of profits to enter all prices, otherwise income distribution is no longer uniquely determined between the 'classes of the community', nor is the structure of relative prices.[1]

Secondly, 'structure of interest rates' implies that all individual rates move up and down together. With rates of profit, as we tried to show, this is not so. Our idea of profits as a permanent income flowing from changing sources is incompatible with the idea of a permanent 'structure' of such flows.

V. STEADY-STATE GROWTH?

Discussions on matters of economic growth have become a favourite pastime of our age. Among newspaper readers and television viewers all over the world, even among some economists, the notion that in this great age of ours it has become possible to sum up in one single figure the result of the economic activity of groups of individuals in countries, regions, or industries, appears to be accepted as a self-evident truth. Such figures are then used as a measure for comparisons over time and, with gusto, between countries.[2] In many circles a low rate of growth of the gross national product has come to be regarded as a symptom of a social *malaise*.

---

[1] A commentator as sympathetic to the Cambridge cause as Professor G. C. Harcourt sadly concludes: 'The weakest, and yet the most vital, link in this chain of reasoning is the assumption of a uniform rate of profits; for, without it, the *relative* price system appears to remain undetermined.' (G. C. Harcourt, *op. cit.*, p. 169n. Italics in original.)

[2] Excellent criticisms are made by Professor G. A. Duncan, 'Growth Delusions', in *Toward Liberty. Essays in honor of Ludwig von Mises*, Institute for Humane Studies, Menlo Park, California, 1971, Vol. I., pp. 276–288.

Politicians have not failed to notice this development and were quick to make the growth rate a weapon in the struggle for power. Perhaps it was inevitable that after the almost universal adoption of full employment as an aim of economic policy, a high growth rate as an election promise should become a powerful political slogan. It has the additional attraction that while employment cannot be fuller than full the growth rate can be higher than 'high'.

The market economy's growth performance has once more become a target of criticism. Marx and Engels in 1847 predicted its impending collapse. 20 years later, in the first volume of *Capital*, Marx tried to show that, in the long run at least, it was not viable. Another 30 years later Marxian revisionism arose and began to shift its ground: capitalism's viability was no longer at issue. That it was incapable of prospering as much as the technical progress it engendered permitted was now to be regarded as its main crime. The tenor of radical criticism of the market economy has not changed much in our time. Nobody can deny that in almost every respect the performance of the market economy of the West in the 20th century has been most impressive. But its critics have never lacked the ingenuity to measure it by standards it must fail to reach. That these standards are largely fictitious may not disturb economists used to dwelling on a high level of abstraction. But it must disturb those manifestly concerned with the real world. It seems to us that in discussing matters of growth the first task of the economist is not to construct ideal types and to describe the location of real growth phenomena by their distance from the ideals, though this may be done *inter alia* later on. His first task is to understand what happens in practice, his second to ask what is technically and economically possible.

We learned above how the Pareto optimum as an ideal type in welfare economics has clouded the judgement of some economists and turned into an obstacle to their understanding of market processes. Something very similar has happened in the theory of growth. Here the notion of 'steady-state growth' has come to occupy the position of the ideal type. We shall endeavour to show, first, the fictitious nature of this notion, secondly, its inadequacy as a fundamental concept of the theory of growth, and, thirdly, the consequent futility of all

[37]

attempts to understand the movement of a growing market economy in terms of it.

Cassel's idea of the 'uniformly progressive economy'

The theory of economic growth has come to occupy a prominent place in economic thought during the last quarter of a century. This development took place in a social climate in which an obsession with the notion of economic growth clouded the judgement of economists and was, of course, influenced by it. But it also had its roots in the history of economic thought. As early as 1911 or 1912 Cassel, dissatisfied with the notion of stationary equilibrium as the basis of the Walrasian system, appears to have conceived the idea of a 'uniformly progressive economy', an economic system in which labour, capital, output and incomes increase annually at a uniform rate, in which all *relative* magnitudes remain constant, output of all goods and services increases at the same rate, and in which all prices therefore remain constant. The idea was evidently re-discovered independently by Sir Roy Harrod in the 1930s.[1]

Growth and macro-formalism

In the macro-economic controversy with which we are concerned growth theory of course plays a prominent part. The neo-classical school hopes to have found here a fertile field in which their theories can undergo statistical verification. The Cambridge School has concentrated its fire on the assumptions on which these theories rest. Adherents of both speak of the 'stylised facts' on which, so they tell us, their views are based. Professor Solow apparently believes that steady-state growth offers a tolerably good approximation to what happens in the market economy.

> 'If it is too much to say that steady-state growth is the normal state of affairs in advanced capitalist economies, it is not too much to say that divergences from steady-state growth appear to be fairly small, casual, and hardly self-accentuating. You would not react to the sight of an economy in steady-state growth as you would react to the sight of a pendulum balanced upside-down, or a vacuum sitting in plain daylight while Nature abhors it.'[2]

[1] 'An Essay in Dynamic Theory', *Economic Journal*, March 1939.
[2] R. M. Solow, *Growth Theory. An Exposition*, op. cit., pp. 11–12.

This is perhaps a less modest claim to make than it appears.

Both schools, then, are concerned with steady-state growth, an equilibrium concept. The equilibrating forces under discussion are macro-economic forces. Some of them we must now regard as suspect: the capital-output ratio, for example, since heterogeneous capital cannot be measured in disequilibrium, or the rate of profit we discussed at length. Again we find that the micro-economic foundations from which these macro-economic forces must be supposed to spring are largely ignored. The possibility of such an equilibrium is discussed at length. The question of *how* it would have to be reached, of the pattern of *action* required for the 'path' that leads towards it, is in general neglected.

Not all plans can succeed

While, then, preoccupation with the state of equilibrium and neglect of the micro-economic roots of macro-economic forces remain characteristic of the style of thought of both rival schools in the economics of growth, we also find that scant attention is paid as a rule to another set of phenomena reflecting subjective attitudes: expectations and plans. In a world of change and growth, one would have thought they must occupy as prominent a place in the thought of the economists interested in it as they do in reality in the thought of the actors. They certainly did in Keynes's thought. But as soon as we ask the simple question: Can all plans succeed?, we realise that the answer, obvious as it may be, holds consequences most dangerous to any notion of macro-economic equilibrium. Walras's Law teaches us that there can be no equilibrium of the economic system as a whole without equilibrium in every *market*. There can be no market equilibrium without equilibrium of each *individual* trading in it. The micro-economic foundation essential to the central macro-economic concept of the two rival schools thus becomes apparent.

No room for individual expectations in macro-economics

Expectations and individual plans play only a minor, if any, part in the arguments of the two schools. In the neo-classical writings they are barely mentioned. Professor Solow, in discussing the social rate of return (his central concept), studiously ignores them. The 'technocratic' approach chosen offers no room for them.

In Professor Joan Robinson's work a certain change has taken place. In 1956, in *The Accumulation of Capital*, expectations were kept at arm's length by the assumption that everybody expects present conditions to last into the future.

'When something occurs which causes a change, we assume that expectations are immediately adjusted, and that no further change is expected.'[1]

In 1971, in *Economic Heresies*, they find occasional mention:

'Instability arises from the influences of current experience upon expectations. When a seller's market is expected to last, it leads to rapid investment which may cause an over-shoot and kill the seller's market. But in a buyer's market, productive capacity is kept in being hoping for a recovery, so that if recovery does not occur, the buyer's market persists'.[2]

Evidently these are not the expectations of individuals, but mass expectations. The scope of the concept as used here is narrowly confined to *identical* expectations held by a large mass of traders. It is simply not wide enough to permit the divergence of expectations held by different individuals, nor to account for its important consequences, such as the equilibrium of asset markets based on a balance of divergent expectations. As nature abhors a vacuum, so our latter-day Cambridge Ricardians abhor the differences between the minds of men.

The Cambridge 'golden age'

Both schools are committed to the notion of steady-state growth, a concept of equilibrium in motion. In the teaching of neo-classical formalism it occupies a central place. The Cambridge School has its own version of it, Mrs Robinson's 'golden age', defined in the following terms:

'With a desired rate of accumulation equal to the possible rate, compounded of the rate of growth of population and of output per head, starting with near full employment and a composition of the stock of plant appropriate to the desired

[1] *Op. cit.*, p. 67.
[2] *Op. cit.*, pp. 22–3.

[40]

rate of accumulation, near full employment is maintained. This is a golden age'.[1]

This equilibrium notion has a number of variants, like 'limping' or 'restrained' golden age, 'leaden age' (equilibrium with unemployment), and various types of 'platinum age'.[2]

Growth equilibrium is equilibrium in motion, equilibrium over time. We have learned from Sir John Hicks to distinguish between equilibrium *at a point of time* and equilibrium *over a period of time*. The former must clearly be an equilibrium resting upon a balance of expectations. On the latter,

> 'If there is to be equilibrium over a period there must be equilibrium at every point of time within the period—an equilibrium which is of course based, as every point-of-time equilibrium must be based, upon its own expectations. But for period equilibrium there is the additional condition that these expectations must be consistent with one another and with what actually happens within the period. Period equilibrium is essential, in dynamic theory, as a standard of reference, but it is hard to see how there can, in general, be any "tendency" to it'.[3]

We are prepared to go one step further. We find it hard to see, not merely how there can be any tendency to it, but how such a thing can be thought to exist at all.

In a stationary world the future is expected to be like the past, but in a world of change the future is unknowable to man. Men have to act on their expectations, make plans accordingly, and try to carry them out. But common experience teaches us that in an uncertain world different men will hold different expectations about events expected to take place at the same future point of time. If so, these expectations cannot all prove right. In each case, at best, one can. The others will prove to have been wrong, and the plans based upon them will fail. In an uncertain world universal success of plans is therefore impossible. *Hence growth equilibrium is impossible.* There can be no general equilibrium over time without equilibrium of each individual participating in it.

[1] Joan Robinson, *Essays in the Theory of Economic Growth*, Macmillan, 1962, p. 52.
[2] *Ibid.*, pp. 53–9.
[3] John Hicks, *Capital and Growth, op. cit.*, p. 24.

Our conclusion is of particular significance for the composition of the stock of capital. In the passage quoted above Mrs Robinson emphasises as a condition of golden-age growth 'a composition of the stock of plant appropriate to the desired rate of accumulation'. This of course is not enough. For equilibrium growth to be possible the composition of the whole capital stock (not merely the 'stock of plant') must at all times be such as to meet all the demands made upon it, not merely for further accumulation but also for use in the production of consumer goods. But where investment plans have to be based upon divergent expectations, some of these plans will be unsuccessful. Hence some malinvestment is inevitable; *but malinvestment is incompatible with equilibrium growth.* Some investment plans will possibly succeed beyond their investors' expectations. These will make capital gains. Other investors will suffer capital losses. Neither gains nor losses are of course compatible with steady-state growth.

It goes without saying that in a one-commodity world there can be no malinvestment and our problem would disappear. Its significance in reality stems from the heterogeneous nature of output in general, and the stock of capital in particular. Specificity and complementarity are of the essence of the matter.

We know from history that a growing economy is not 'uniformly progressive' in Cassel's sense. The composition of consumption output demanded, for example, will change. As people grow richer they will demand some goods they have not had before. They may reduce their demand for other goods they have now come to regard as inferior. And the demand for many will rise, but at a different rate for each good.

These shifts in demand accompanying growth cannot be predicted. If all capital were homogeneous ('malleable' is the term used in these discussions), capital would be shifted, in a Ricardian fashion, out of industries in which demand is slack into industries in which demand is buoyant. In the real world in which capital goods are mostly durable and specific, such capital movements between industries are possible only on a small scale. The composition of the capital stock as determined by the investment plans of past and present will therefore be different from the composition as required by the structure of present commodity demand. The capital stock will never have its equilibrium composition. But without it there can be no steady-state growth.

Equilibrium growth is a misconception

We must conclude that the concept of equilibrium growth is a misconception. It would require a world of convergent expectations all of which are invariably fulfilled and, resting upon them, of individual plans all of which are consistent with one another. Walrasian general equilibrium makes sense only in a stationary world in which expectations play no part that could be called economically significant, and in which all plans of households and firms, attuned to the same set of existing prices, are consistent.

The real world of the market economy with its divergent expectations, inconsistent plans and competitive markets (not of course in the text-book sense), with its malinvestment and its take-over bids made by those who can see more profitable uses of malinvested capital than its existing owners and managers, is an altogether different place from that envisaged by the macro-economists. Even to speak here of an 'approach to equilibrium' by *tâtonnement* (a process of trial and error) is rather misleading. The nature of the equilibrium constellation, if there be one, would continuously change as old plans are discarded and new expectations, divergent and unpredictable by their very nature, are formed. It is not surprising that our latter-day Ricardians should find most uncongenial a world in which different men, in the same 'objective situation', act differently and thus with unequal success, and that they should wish to escape, as Professor Joan Robinson does, into altogether different worlds of various metallic compositions. Nor that the neo-classical formalists wish to take refuge in a world which, while it has been made up to look like the real world of unpredictable change, yet permits them to ply their trade with their familiar tools.

There can be no such 'in-between' world. We have to choose between the stationary state and the real world in which market processes have to be described and interpreted without much benefit of the inventory of equilibrium tools. There always are equilibrium forces, but there also are disequilibrating forces engendered by unexpected change. On many occasions the latter are likely to overtake the former.

[43]

VI. THE DISEQUILIBRATING FORCE OF TECHNICAL PROGRESS

One such disequilibrating force is continuous technical progress, a characteristic feature of the industrial society of the West and perhaps the strongest element in the economic growth processes we observe in it. How can this disequilibrating force be reconciled with macro-economic equilibrium? Since it is a force emanating from human endeavour in hundreds of laboratories and thousands of workshops, how can a place for it be found within a system of macro-variables?

Dangerous thoughts

Professor Robinson, perspicacious and candid as ever, sees the problem and, for one fleeting moment, even draws our attention to it.

'There is something contradictory in postulating a uniform rate of profit throughout an economy in which technical progress is going on. Some firms are always taking advantage of new ideas faster than others and enjoying a higher rate of profit in their investments. Moreover, technical progress alters the nature of commodities and the requirements of skill and training of workers.'[1]

No such admission, to our knowledge, is ever to be found in neo-classical writings. But such dangerous thoughts are no sooner given expression by this eminent macro-economist than they are brushed aside.

'However, there does not seem to be much hope of dealing with such problems until the main lines of a simplified analysis have been established. We therefore make the drastic assumptions that commodities and workers retain their physical characteristics and all technical change is concentrated in the design of equipment.'

The reader must note that 'simplified analysis' means here 'in macro-economic terms'. It does not mean, what after all it might mean, 'in terms of the fundamental elements of which it is composed in reality', such as desires and expectations.

[1] *Economic Heresies*, op. cit., p. 128.

Technical progress was at first treated by economists as a force originating outside the economic system and impinging upon it, modifying output quantities and prices. Soon it was realised that this is an untenable assumption for modern society. Its creation and diffusion have become regular economic activities. It was also realised that *specifying investment decisions*[1] are affected by it.

For macro-economic formalism technical progress poses several problems: how to give it a respectable macro-form, and how to turn it into an equilibrating force which fits into its equilibrium system. The latter, in particular, was no easy task: general equilibrium requires general knowledge while technical progress implies more or less continuous change in knowledge. We shall see how the need to formalise human knowledge and its modes of change, which defy all such attempts, has produced some odd results.

Here the Cambridge School scored a success when Professor Nicholas Kaldor introduced his *technical progress function*[2]

'which makes the annual rate of growth of productivity per worker *operating on new equipment* a function of the rate of growth of investment per worker'.[3] (His italics.)

In this way he contrived to turn the results of technical progress into a macro-variable, a dependent variable of gross investment. This approach appeared to entail some interesting conclusions. We are told that

'The main "practical" conclusion for economic policy that emerges from this model is that any scheme leading to the accelerated retirement of old equipment (such as a tax on the use of obsolete plant and equipment) is bound to accelerate for a temporary period the rate of increase in output per head.'[4]

---

[1] 'Glossary', p. 9.
[2] 'Glossary', p. 10.
[3] N. Kaldor and J. A. Mirrlees, 'A New Model of Economic Growth', reprinted in A. Sen (ed.), *Growth Economics*, Penguin Modern Economics Readings, Penguin Books, 1970, p. 346.
[4] *Ibid.*, p. 366.

This is followed by a call for

> 'higher-quality business management which is more alert in searching for technical improvements and less resistant to their introduction'.

'Learning by doing'

It will be readily appreciated why the wide recognition which *learning by doing*[1] as an important form of technical progress has gained in recent years has caused acute embarrassment to macro-economic formalism. When workers gradually learn from experience how to handle their equipment more efficiently and thus improve their productivity, *the link with gross investment is broken*, and the attempt to restore it by the assumption that it takes exclusively the form of workers in the capital goods industries learning by producing their various 'machines', only serves to underline its highly artificial character.[2] There is no reason why most of what is to be learned here should not be learned by the use of such 'machines' in the production of consumer goods rather than in the course of their own production, which, it is clear, means the use of other existing capital resources. It is no doubt possible to formalise this process of 'learning by doing' by making it simply a (possibly declining) function of time. The point causing embarrassment is that the productive results of the use of equipment may well be both a function of gross investment *and* a function of time. As long as output gains can be derived from the *longer* use of existing equipment, contrary to Professor Kaldor's view, delay in its replacement may be justified; it all depends on where the larger net gains can be made. On this, in each concrete case, opinions may differ. In the market economy such difference of opinions finds its expression in some firms keeping their old equipment longer than others.

Technical progress is unpredictable

We have now reached what really is the crux of the matter. Macro-economic formalism of both persuasions has to treat as *fact* what, at the time at which the relevant decisions have to

---

[1] 'Glossary', p. 9.
[2] As long as only workers in capital goods industries can 'learn by doing' the link with gross investment is maintained since their output equals gross investment and the more they produce the more they presumably 'learn'.

be taken, must still be *opinion*. It is now fairly generally agreed that some technical progress requires new equipment while some may be derived from improved use of existing equipment, that technical progress may be either 'embodied' or 'disembodied'.[1] If 'embodied' (incorporated in specific machines), when we have shown that gross investment is a necessary condition of embodied progress we have not yet shown it to be a sufficient condition. Which changes in the design of equipment will turn out to be improvements is not known at the moment the specifying investment decision has to be made; only practical experience can tell. Malinvestment is always possible. However alert a manager may be to the introduction of new equipment, he may yet make disastrous mistakes. *Not every technical change is tantamount to technical progress.*

This can be seen even more clearly if, disregarding Professor Robinson's 'drastic assumptions', we include product innovation together with process innovation in our concept of technical progress. When a new product is introduced nobody can tell whether its production and sale will be profitable, whether the market will absorb it in sufficient quantities. Even less does anybody know, if the condition is met, how long it will last, or how soon another firm may put a superior version of it on the market. Only manifold experience in workshop and household (in domestic equipment) can show which of the many technically possible changes are real improvements.

Markets are 'the final arbiter'

In a market economy decisions to innovate and the corresponding specifying investment decisions are decentralised, with the result that such individual plans will inevitably become inconsistent. It is the market which in the end decides upon success and failure, i.e., which changes constitute 'progress' and which 'regress'. Decentralisation in the first stage of the process of change, which permits a vast amount of knowledge to be gathered by the planners of inconsistent plans, is followed, once all the knowledge to be gathered is available, by the final decision of the market, acting here as the decision-making agent of society.

It goes without saying that in the case of 'learning by doing', where no investment decisions are involved, we reach the same

---

[1] 'Glossary', p. 10.

conclusion. Different men learn different lessons from doing the same work. What is more, even those who learn similar lessons will apply them in different directions. We find again decentralisation at the first stage at which new knowledge is gathered, and in the end the market as the final arbiter of what constitutes 'progress'.

It may be that after a time only one type of the new product, or one type of a new design of the equipment, is left in the market. It is clear, we trust, that such a 'state of equilibrium' would mark the (temporary) end of the process of technical progress. What constitutes progress we can know only when it is no longer taking place.

Professor Kaldor, in exhorting his managers to be 'more alert in searching for technical improvements and less resistant to their introduction', did not suggest that the search would always be successful. But it is neither always clear what constitutes an improvement nor, provided this question can be answered, certain that an even bigger improvement to-morrow may not reward those willing to wait. It is hard to derive useful recipes for concrete action from macro-economic generalisations.

We hope to have shown why macro-economic formalism is incapable of doing justice to the phenomena of technical progress in a market economy. The simultaneous pursuit of new knowledge by rival agents in terms of mutually inconsistent plans is not amenable to generalisations in general equilibrium terms, while the terms of its vocabulary—'output per man on new equipment' or 'gross investment per worker'— have no identifiable counterpart in reality.

VII. CONCLUSIONS FOR ECONOMIC POLICY AND THE FUNCTIONING OF THE MARKET ECONOMY

From what we have said there follow some conclusions for economic policy.

1. *Incomes policy*

In many countries an incomes policy is today advocated as the only remaining remedy for the permanent inflation of our age. Such a policy, however, by putting the price mechanism out of action, would deprive the market of its main function. It implies the control of all prices and incomes and must, in the end, lead to the central direction of all economic activity.

We might add that such a policy would give rise to quite unmanageable problems in the determination of profit margins on the various goods. We saw above that the flow of profits in a market economy is a permanent flow from ever-changing sources. How is it to be reconciled with an incomes policy the main purpose of which is to 'freeze' an existing relative price and income structure? And even if this were possible, who is to decide on the sequence of changing sources of profits?

2. *Economic growth*

After what we have said above about growth as the cumulative result of the actions of millions of individuals, it should be clear that 'growth targets' cannot be aims of economic policy and projected growth rates of GNP are meaningless. In most cases, of course, growth policy is simply a euphemism for more inflation. Where, however, it means the 'co-ordination of expectations' with the aim of reducing their divergence, and making them all converge on a single 'target growth rate', as is the case with 'indicative planning', we have to ask who is to determine it and on the basis of what. Controlling expectations is as incompatible with the market economy as is price control.

3. *Technical progress*

We have tried to show why 'accelerated retirement of old equipment' may not always benefit society in the short run. In the long run the conclusion that we have to look for 'business management which is more alert in searching for technical improvements and less resistant to their introduction' does not always hold. Technical change need not mean technical progress.

4. *Main conclusions*

The main conclusion for economic policy, however, to which our argument leads, must be that the terms in which contemporary economists usually conduct discussions on matters of economic policy, such as growth or fiscal policy, are misleading.

(i) *Macro-aggregates*

Growth is only one kind of economic change, albeit an important one. It is not a kind of change that could take place in isolation from others. Aggregates, such as gross domestic product or gross investment in manufacturing industries, are therefore not to be regarded as magnitudes which would or could remain constant but for growth. Their composition is undergoing continuous change affecting their total magnitude. Growth of the aggregates is always the cumulative result of other changes in quantities of resources and factor productivity, in relative prices and demand, and so on. Only in a one-commodity world could it be otherwise.

It is therefore impossible to discuss meaningfully policy measures designed to affect the magnitude of such aggregates without also discussing those changes in their composition which must accompany them.

Perhaps an historical example will elucidate what we mean. Policies based on Keynesian macro-economic recipes might have succeeded (had they then been tried) in 1932 and did succeed in 1940 because it so happened that at the bottom of the Great Depression as well as during the Second World War all sectors of the economy were equally affected. In 1932 any kind of additional spending on whatever kind of goods would have had a favourable effect on incomes because there was unemployment everywhere, as well as idle capital equipment and surplus stocks of raw materials. During the war the situation was exactly the opposite, but precisely for this reason the same recipes, but with opposite sign, applied. With millions of men and women in the armed forces everything, not merely labour, was scarce and any reduction in demand anywhere welcome.

These are, of course, abnormal situations. Normally in an industrial economy we find some declining industries (coal mining, cinemas) side by side with rapidly expanding ones. Problems arising here require detailed study and are resistant to macro-economic panaceas.

(ii) *Monetary policy*

In monetary policy, however, these conclusions do not hold without certain qualifications and reservations. In matters of money the character of the relationships between macro-economic magnitudes and the individual acts of choice that govern them is far more complex than elsewhere.

The quantity of money is a macro-economic magnitude which has always occupied a prominent place in economic thought. Where it consists of gold and silver the micro-foundation is somewhat remote, and the same applies to a paper money created by government authority. In this context two problems call for particular notice.

First, while the supply of money may sometimes be regarded as a social datum, the demand for it flows from acts of choice (liquidity preference), as Keynes taught and the Chicago School acknowledges. Secondly, the well-known difficulty in distinguishing between money and credit adds to the complexity of our problem. The volume of credit, continuously fluctuating as old loans are repaid and new loans granted, is of course fairly closely linked to creditors' and debtors' choice. The various components of the total supply of money and credit are thus seen to have links of various degrees of proximity to their micro-foundations. In our world the total supply is probably more closely so linked than it was 100 years ago. In discussions on monetary policy these considerations should not be overlooked. The success of a monetary policy must always depend, to a large extent, on whether the volume of credit will move in the same, or an opposite, direction as the money supply determined by policy-makers.

Whatever the deeper causes of the sustained criticisms of the market economy we witness in our day, some have to be ascribed to the picture of it we find in the writings of contemporary economists. We repeat that there can be no question of calling any one kind of perspective in which the market economy may be viewed the 'right' one. A large number of such perspectives is possible, indeed desirable. But it is true that some approaches are inadequate to their subject matter since their conceptual tools do not permit those who handle them to grapple with important features of the subject.

(iii) *Cambridge School*
Neo-Ricardians of the Cambridge School are, by their own admission, not interested in *relative* quantities and prices, let alone in the preferences and expectations that govern them. They are therefore ill-equipped to deal with autonomous changes in demand or in the range of divergence of expectations, to which Keynes attributed importance and drew our attention, and on which the pattern of specifying investment decisions depends. It is hard to see what their style of thought can contribute to our understanding of the ways in which the

[51]

market economy functions, in particular of its growth patterns. Macro-economic theories without micro-economic substructure are bound to rest upon rather hollow foundations.

(iv) *Neo-classical School*

The adherents of the style of thought we call 'neo-classical formalism', today the predominant school of economic thought in the Western world, are hardly better equipped to make us understand what happens in a market economy. To be sure, from time to time they acknowledge the existence of the micro-foundations, but in reality, as we saw, these perfunctory affirmations are of no significance. The micro-foundations are in their work so hopelessly formalised, technical change stylised as change in productivity of given inputs, preferences regarded as immutable, expectations altogether ignored, that the economic phenomena of this sphere are rendered sterile. The really important variables in their models appear to be quite impervious to the operation of any forces emanating from the micro-sphere. The macro-economic theories of neo-classical formalism may appear to their authors to rest securely on micro-foundations; *they certainly do not have their roots there.*

A good deal of the contemporary misapprehension of, and hostility to, the market economy is thus the economists' fault.

All economic theory must ultimately be related to facts. Professors Kaldor and Solow have on occasion enumerated what they regard as 'stylised facts' governing the situation of modern industrial economies. It seems to us that the following are even more important facts, though in modern discussions such as those we reported on they seem as often as not to be ignored.

(v) *Labour, capital, and expectations*

Labour, in the sense of hours of work done, has by itself no economic value. It has such value when devoted to the rendering of services for which there is a demand. The activity of directing labour to the production of useful, and not useless, objects is therefore an important economic function.

The value of capital goods and titles to them (securities) is governed not by their cost of production, not therefore by *past* labour (bygones are bygones), but by *future* income streams expected to flow from combining them. Expectations always differ between men. In a market economy there is a central

[52]

market for shares in capital combinations, the Stock Exchange, in which the prices of these shares, governed by a balance of expectations between 'bulls' and 'bears', is fixed anew every day. As this balance of expectations tilts from day to day, so do prices. It is the existence of the Stock Exchange, and not the respective magnitudes of the 'private' and 'public' sectors, which characteristically distinguishes a market economy from a socialist one.

All economic activity consists in making, carrying out and revising plans. In a market economy every one has to solve problems, and no two people solve theirs in precisely the same way. No two consumers have identical tastes. No two housewives with the same amounts of housekeeping money spend them in identical fashion. Over time, of course, the composition of these bundles of goods changes even for the same household.

The mere change of generations, if not that of human moods, thus causes continuous change in the composition of aggregates. Economic growth is nothing but a by-product of these continuous and fundamental changes. We cannot understand growth if we abstract from them.

In the same way, every firm is different from every other. Each has a capital combination (buildings, machines, stocks of materials) not exactly identical with that of any other. A dozen machine tools, physically alike, may well be used in a dozen different firms to serve different markets. Firms may learn from each other's successes and failures. The unsuccessful may emulate the successful, they may exchange information in various ways, but important differences always remain.

In a market economy there are thus always some forces making for similarity by competition and emulation, but also others making for dissimilarity by innovation. The former can never wipe out the latter, and even the pattern of similarity changes all the time.

There can be no systematic thought on anything without a measure of abstraction. Thus, at some stage, we have to abstract from these individual differences. We may, then, speak of consumption patterns and the composition of the gross domestic product. We have no right to assume that these aggregates can, over time, lead a life of their own. All the time they will be shaped and re-shaped by forces emanating from the microsphere, forces that ultimately stem from human choice and decision.

[53]

SUGGESTED QUESTIONS FOR DISCUSSION

1. What precisely do we mean when we speak of 'macro-economic formalism'?

2. 'Profits are a permanent income flowing from variable sources.' Elucidate.

3. What economic forces prevent a 'uniform rate of profit' from coming into existence?

4. Why can there be no such thing as 'equilibrium growth'?

5. Trace some of the consequences, for the planning and success of economic action, of a divergence of expectations.

6. What would a world have to look like in which all plans were to succeed?

7. Explain the nature and consequences of malinvestment.

8. 'We can never tell which technical change constitutes technical progress before it has been superseded by another change.' Discuss the implications of this statement.

9. Why must an 'incomes policy' fail in the long run?

10. 'Economic growth is one kind of change among many. We have no right to assume that at any time it is the only kind to occur.' Comment.

FURTHER READING

Bronfenbrenner, Martin, *Income Distribution Theory*, Aldine, New York, 1971.

Ferguson, C. E., *Neoclassical Theory of Production and Distribution*, Cambridge University Press, 1969.

Fisher, Irving, *The Theory of Interest*, The Macmillan Co., New York, 1930.

Dewey, Donald, *Modern Capital Theory*, Columbia University Press, New York, 1965.

Hayek, Friedrich A., *Profits, Interest and Investment*, Routledge & Kegan Paul, London, 1939.

Hicks, John, *Capital and Growth*, Oxford University Press, London, 1965.

Kaldor, Nicholas, *Essays on Economic Stability and Growth*, Duckworth, London, 1960.

Kirzner, Israel M., *An Essay on Capital*, Kelley, New York, 1966.

Knight, Frank H., *Risk, Uncertainty and Profit*, London School of Economics, 1933.
— *On the History and Method of Economics*, University of Chicago Press, Chicago, 1956.

Lachmann, L. M., *Capital and its Structure*, Bell, London, 1956.

Ricardo, David, *Principles of Political Economy and Taxation*, London, 1817.

Robinson, Joan, *The Accumulation of Capital*, Macmillan, London, 1956.
— *Essays in the Theory of Economic Growth*, Macmillan, London, 1962.

Samuelson, Paul, *Foundations of Economic Analysis*, Harvard University Press, Cambridge, Mass., 1947.

Schumpeter, Joseph A., *The Theory of Economic Development*, Harvard University Press, Cambridge, Mass., 1934.

Sen, Amartya (ed.), *Growth Economics*, Penguin Modern Economics Readings, Penguin Books, 1970.

Solow, Robert M., *Capital and the Rate of Return*, North Holland Publishing, Amsterdam, 1963.

— *Growth Theory*, Oxford University Press, London, 1970.

Sraffa, Piero, *Production of Commodities by Means of Commodities. Prelude to a Critique of Economic Theory*, Cambridge University Press, 1960.